The Discovery Books are prepared

under the educational supervision of

Mary C. Austin, Ed.D.

Reading Specialist and

Professor of Education

Western Reserve University

A DISCOVERY BOOK

GARRARD PUBLISHING COMPANY
CHAMPAIGN, ILLINOIS

U. S. Grant

Horseman and Fighter

by Colonel Red Reeder
illustrated by Ken Wagner

This book is for

Russell Reeder Campion

Contents

U. S. Grant: Horseman and Fighter

CHAPTER

1   The Circus 7

2   What Does U. S. Stand For?   15

3   High Jinks and High Jumps   21

4   Courage 27

5   Hard Times 37

6   Back in Uniform 42

7   Sam Wins 47

8   Sam's Bold Idea 52

9   Sam Wins Again 59

10   U. S. Grant and Robert E. Lee   65

11   President Sam Grant . . . 74

Chapter *1*

The Circus

A man in the circus ring shouted, "Ladies and gentlemen! I will give anyone five dollars who can ride this horse."

The horse pranced around the ring to the tune of the circus band. He had neither reins nor saddle. His back was shiny and slippery from a coat of grease. The animal looked peaceful but he was dangerous. He had been taught to buck off any rider.

A boy decided to try for the money. As he mounted the horse, a clown cracked a whip. The horse tossed his head and trotted around the ring. The faster the band played, the faster the horse ran. Suddenly, the band stopped. The horse bucked the boy off. Everyone laughed.

Eleven-year-old Ulysses Grant stood up. "I can ride that horse," he said. His gray eyes flashed. "May I try, Mother?"

Mrs. Grant smiled. She called him by his nickname. *"Lys, you have a way with horses. I think you can ride him."*

The band stopped when Lys entered the ring. Though Lys was plump, he was small for his age. On the back of the horse he looked even smaller.

He gripped the horse tightly with his knees.

The band played a waltz. Lys patted the horse's neck. When the band played faster, the horse galloped. Suddenly, the band stopped and the trick horse stopped. He arched his back quickly and kicked up his rear heels. Lys hardly moved. Everyone clapped.

"Give him the money!" the crowd yelled. Lys took the money and slid from the animal's back.

Quietly he went back to his seat. His younger brother and sister jumped up and down. They were proud of Lys.

His father was proud, too, when he learned the news that evening.

Mr. Grant was fond of his oldest child. "You're the best rider in Georgetown!" he said.

Farmers for miles around heard about Lys's riding the trick horse. They brought their wild young colts to Lys to train.

The farmland around Georgetown, Ohio, had been settled only recently. Lys had been born in Point Pleasant, Ohio, in 1822. His family moved to nearby Georgetown one year later.

Mr. Grant owned a tannery. Here skins of animals were made into leather. Sometimes Lys had to help in the tannery. He hated the work. The smell of the bloody animal skins and of the acids used to cure them made him feel sick.

Mr. Grant also owned a stable. Lys didn't have to be asked to work there! He drove big teams of horses to the woods. He brought back loads of bark to the tannery. Acids from the bark were used in curing the leather. He also taught his little sisters and brothers to ride. There were two brothers and three sisters.

Travelers often rented Mr. Grant's horses. Lys sometimes drove them to towns nearby.

One day when Lys was thirteen his father called him to the stable. "Lys, these two men want to go to Toledo. I told them you will take them."

Lys's eyes shone with excitement. Toledo was 200 miles away!

It was a long, hard trip across country. The roads were rough. The bridges were few. Lys had to drive the horses safely through the streams.

They made it to Toledo in good time. "You did a man's job, boy, and you did it well," one of the men said, clapping Lys on the back. "Tell your Pa you've got a good head on your shoulders."

Chapter *2*

What Does U. S. Stand For?

When Lys became seventeen, his father said to him, "Ulysses, how would you like to go to West Point and be a cadet?"

Lys knew that West Point was the United States Military Academy. Cadets were trained there to become Army officers. Lys wasn't sure he wanted to be in the Army. Still he longed to travel. This would be a chance.

"I would like to go," Ulysses said.

"I can arrange it," his father said. "I want you to have an education."

The time came to go. Lys dressed in his best suit. He was still short for his age, but he was thin and wiry. He felt strange as he kissed his mother good-by. When he reached the Ohio River his spirits rose. It was thrilling being on a steamboat.

In Pennsylvania, he took his first railroad train. Lys felt important to be on his own.

He visited Philadelphia and New York City. Then he took a Hudson River boat for West Point. It was summer. West Point was beautiful. Old Fort Putnam, high on a hill, seemed to guard the military school.

When Grant reported there he changed his name. His father had named him "Hiram Ulysses Grant." Lys was often teased, as the initials spelled HUG. So he turned his name around to "Ulysses Hiram Grant."

An officer said, "We are expecting a 'Ulysses Simpson Grant' from Ohio."

"I am Grant from Ohio. But my name is not 'Ulysses Simpson Grant.' "

The officer scratched his head. There was a mistake in the papers from Washington. "You can enter the Academy, but only as 'Ulysses Simpson Grant,' " the officer said.

"All right," the boy agreed.

He liked the initials U. S. G. They could stand for "United States" Grant. They could also stand for "Uncle Sam."

Because of this, the cadets called him Sam.

At first, Sam found cadet life hard. He felt as if he could do nothing right. In the summer, the cadets lived in tents. Sam's tent was not neat enough to suit the officers. Reports on the bulletin board told of his many mistakes.

Sam Grant was discouraged. He missed his family. But he did not quit.

In the fall when classes started Sam liked West Point better. He enjoyed mathematics and studied hard.

Sam did not like to parade. Few cadets did. The parades seemed a waste of time. But one day the cadets heard they were to parade for General Winfield Scott.

"I will like that," Sam said.

Every cadet knew about Scott, hero of the War of 1812. Scott was a giant. His blue uniform, with its gold buttons and red sash, made him look even bigger. A long sword hung at his waist. He was the senior general of the Army.

When the band played, Sam's company swept by in full dress uniform. Flags rippled in the breeze. Every cadet was marching his best.

When Sam saw General Scott, he said to himself, "Some day I will come back to see the cadets parade. Some day I will be the head of the Army." This was Sam's secret. He told no one.

Chapter 3

High Jinks and
High Jumps

When Sam had been at West Point a year, he and another cadet played a daring prank.

One dark night, Sam and Cadet George DeShon left their room. They crept toward the yard of Lieutenant Smith, the officer in charge of cadets. Sam and George took one of the officer's turkeys and ran for the barracks.

The two boys cooked the turkey over the fireplace. It cooked slowly.

The boys knew that if they were caught they would be sent home.

The turkey smelled delicious. Just as it was done, an officer knocked on the door. The two cadets sprang to attention in front of the fire.

"Good evening," the officer said.

"Good evening, sir," the cadets replied.

The officer sniffed the air. The boys hardly breathed. Grant's gray eyes looked straight to the front. His freckled face did not show he was nervous.

When the officer left, the cadets ate the turkey as fast as they could. The officer did not report them.

"I can't understand how we escaped," Cadet DeShon said.

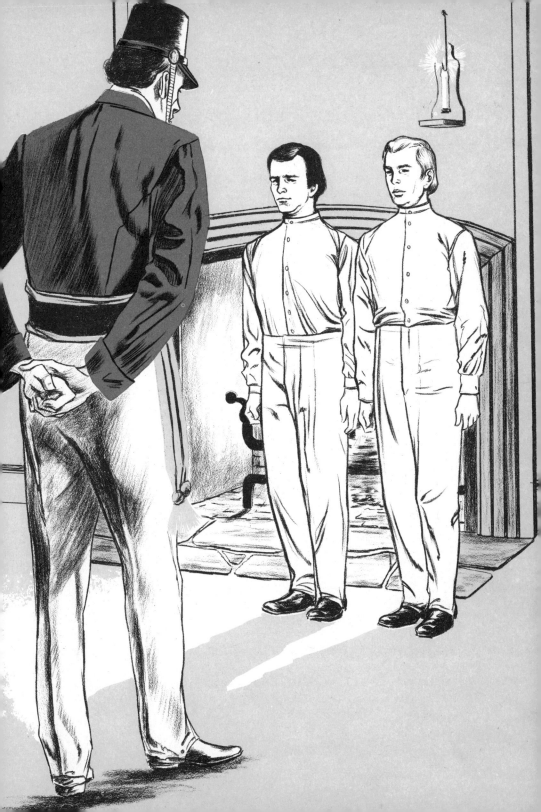

The cadets had better ways of enjoying themselves. Almost all of them liked horseback riding. During his last year at West Point, Sam was the best rider of all. He was fearless.

At graduation time, people came to see the cadets ride. Sam got ready to jump a horse named York. "Put the bar up as high as it can go," he said.

"Watch out!" a cadet warned. "A jump that high is dangerous. If York trips on the bar you'll be killed."

Sam looked tiny as he swung into York's saddle. He galloped the powerful horse to the end of the indoor ring. York pawed the ground.

Suddenly, Grant kicked his heels against York's sides. They raced for the bar. The jump looked impossible. The big horse gave a leap. Grant and York shot through the air. They cleared the bar! Everyone cheered.

Sam hated to leave West Point. It was not only beautiful, but it had also taught him many things. He knew how to take care of soldiers now, and how to lead them.

Orders came for Sam to go to Jefferson Barracks, near St. Louis, Missouri. Cadet Fred Dent had been one of Sam's roommates. "My family lives near there," Fred said. "Please come to visit. We have some fine horses and I have a sister, Julia, who is very pretty. She's a fine rider."

Chapter *4*

Courage

Lieutenant Sam Grant and some other officers taught the soldiers at Jefferson Barracks how to shoot and march. In his spare time Sam rode his horse.

One day he rode out in the country to the Dent family's house.

Mrs. Dent was nice to Sam. She made him feel as if he were one of her boys. "Our daughter, Julia," Mrs. Dent said, "is away at school."

When Julia returned, Sam liked her at once. The seventeen-year-old girl had her mother's way of making friends. Sam came to the Dent home often to talk with Julia. He and Julia enjoyed walking and riding in the woods. They were together as much as possible.

A year went by. One day when Sam came to see Julia, he looked worried.

"What is the matter?" Julia asked anxiously.

"Our regiment is ordered away," Sam said. "There is going to be a war with Mexico."

Julia's blue eyes flashed. "You told me you did not believe it right to fight the Mexicans."

Sam looked sadder than Julia had ever seen him. "I think it is wrong to fight a weak country and take its land," he said. "The United States wants Texas, because many Americans live there. But Mexico owns Texas and won't let it go."

Julia frowned. "What are you going to do?"

"I came to tell you good-by," he said. "It is my duty to go with my regiment." Sam's heart raced. "I do not want to leave you."

It was a hard moment for both of them. Before Sam left, he and Julia became engaged to be married.

"I'll wait for you," Julia promised.

"I'll come back," Sam said.

They both knew danger lay ahead.

On the march into Mexico, Sam was placed in charge of a mule pack train. The mules walked at the rear of the army. Sam still felt sorry for the Mexicans. But as long as the war had started, he wanted to see action.

"Sir," Sam told his colonel, "I want to be a fighter."

Colonel Garland shook his head. "No," he said. "You stay back and run the supply train."

This was dull work. Sam had to buy food for the Army. Then he had to see that it was packed up each morning, along with the tents and other supplies. Often the mules bucked off their loads. Other times they rolled in the dirt, trying to mash them.

Sometimes they refused to walk. Sometimes they even ran away. It took all of Sam's patience to keep 2,000 mules going.

The United States Army won its first battles easily. But when it marched deeper into Mexico, things got more difficult.

The city of Monterrey was guarded by forts. A hard battle started there. Sam could not bear to be left out of the battle. "Take care of the mules," he told a sergeant. "I want to see what's going on."

Sam found Colonel Garland. He had ordered his men to charge a fort. Sam and his horse joined the charge.

They were beaten back. They attacked the city from another point.

They captured a bridge and fought their way slowly down the city streets. Each street was blocked by logs or fences. Bullets came from the rooftops, where Mexican snipers lay. Cannon balls came hurtling from the forts. Many men were wounded.

The fight became harder and harder. Garland's men had little ammunition.

"We need some ammunition badly," Colonel Garland said. "Someone has to go back for it. Who will go?"

Everyone knew that the man who went would be in great danger.

Sam held up his hand. "I will go," he said.

Sam was on a gray horse. He tightened his saddle girth. But he did not sit in the horse's saddle.

He fastened himself, crab-like, to the side of the animal. He started the horse at a run.

At each street corner, bullets cracked about the horse and Sam. At the last corner, a four foot wall blocked the way. Sam clung tighter to the horse. The animal jumped over the wall.

Sam worked fast to gather the ammunition. But before he got it together, the soldiers came running back from the city. However, other soldiers attacked Monterrey from the west. The next morning Monterrey surrendered.

Everyone talked of Sam's courage. Sam did not act as if he had done anything brave.

The war dragged on. It seemed to Sam as if it would never end. But he was learning about war, and he saw how the generals ran the army.

One day, Sam met Captain Robert E. Lee. Lee was famous because he scouted alone. He rode far ahead of the army. Captain Lee paid no attention to young Lieutenant Grant. Years later he would, when they met again.

The first thing Sam did when the war ended was to go to see Julia Dent. He had been gone four years. When Sam galloped up to Julia's house, he felt more nervous than when he had ridden to get ammunition at Monterrey.

Chapter *5*

Hard Times

Sam and Julia had a beautiful wedding. They went to live near Lake Ontario, where Sam's regiment was stationed.

Their first baby, Frederick, was born. Four happy years went by. Then Lieutenant Grant's regiment was ordered to the Pacific Coast. "I hate to leave you and little Fred," he told Julia. "The trip is dangerous. You two must go to live with my family or yours."

In Oregon, Sam and the other soldiers lived in a fort on the Columbia River. This was wild country. Sam soon tired of drilling and other routines of a peacetime army. He missed his family.

A letter from Julia told of another baby being born. Sam felt more lonely than ever. He worried because he had little money to send home.

Two years dragged by. Orders came from Washington making Sam a captain. But he decided to leave the Army. "I miss my family too much," he said.

Sam traveled to St. Louis. He was thrilled to be home. He worked all summer cutting down trees to build a cabin for Julia and their children.

Soon they had four children. To make money for them, Sam planted potatoes, wheat, and corn. Frost ruined the crops. Things looked black.

Sam sold his farm and his horses. He went to work selling land. But he was a poor salesman. He seemed to do nothing right. Mr. Grant said, *"West Point trained Sam for the Army. It ruined him for business."*

But Sam did not stop trying. He looked for work as an engineer. "I learned to lay out roads at West Point," he said to Julia. He walked the streets, but he found no job.

Sam's father told him that he could be a clerk in his leather store.

Sam moved his family to Galena, Illinois. He worked hard in the store.

On trips and in the store, he heard arguments about slavery. The Northern states wanted to stop slavery. The Southern states did not.

"Slavery is wrong," one man said.

"I see no harm in it," another cried. "I'm from the South. If we cannot have slaves, my state will leave the Union."

"That would bring war!" the first man shouted. He turned to Sam. "What do you think?"

"Slavery is wrong and so is war," said Sam quietly. "But we must hold the United States together, even if it means war."

It was hard for Sam to imagine that the United States could break up. But the country seemed closer to war.

Chapter 6

Back in Uniform

Sam was 39 when the Civil War started in 1861. There was great excitement. President Lincoln called for 75,000 men. He was determined to keep the Union together.

Sam loved the United States. "It is my duty to help my country," he told Julia.

Sam wrote a letter to Army headquarters in Washington, D.C. But no answer came. So Sam went to Cincinnati to see General McClellan.

Sam wanted a job in the Army. The general was too busy to see him.

Sam felt bad. He sat on the porch of his father's store. A wagon in the street was stuck in the mud. "I am like that wagon," he said.

Finally, the Governor of Illinois heard of Sam Grant. The Governor said, "Grant, I will make you a colonel. Do you think you can lead a regiment?"

"I know I can," Sam said.

When Sam met his regiment, the soldiers laughed at him. He had no uniform. His coat had holes at the elbows. He wore a red handkerchief at his waist instead of an officer's red sash. He carried a stick instead of a sword. He did have a fine horse.

Sam loved to ride Jack, who was the color of cream.

"Who is this funny little man?" the soldiers howled.

The soldiers soon stopped laughing. They found they had to behave. If they were late for a march, Sam took away their food.

A friend loaned Sam money to buy a uniform. Sam drilled his soldiers hard. The regiment improved. Sam was promoted to general.

He heard that Southern soldiers were at Belmont, Missouri. This was on the banks of the Mississippi River. Sam decided to attack at once.

In the battle, the Northern soldiers seemed to be winning at first. Sam rode Jack along the battle lines.

Then more Southern soldiers arrived. The Northern soldiers ran to the river. They climbed into boats to get away.

The last boat got ready to leave. Men worked to untie the lines that held it. Then they saw Sam, still on the river bank. He had waited until the last to make sure everyone was safe.

"Go ahead," Sam called. "Cut your lines."

Sam made Jack slide down the slippery bank. Someone put out a plank. Jack walked up it to the deck. The soldiers cheered. They were proud of Grant.

Chapter 7

Sam Wins

Many of President Lincoln's generals seemed afraid to fight. Time and again they asked for more soldiers and more time before they would attack. This worried the President.

Sam was different. When he heard that the Southerners had built two forts in Tennessee, he wanted to capture them.

Fort Henry was on the Tennessee River. Fort Donelson was on the Cumberland River. Sam heard that the Southerners were making the forts stronger. He saddled his new horse, Fox, and rode to see General Halleck.

"I want to attack Fort Henry," said Sam.

"You cannot do it," Halleck replied. "You are too bold."

"I can take the fort," Sam said.

Finally, the general agreed.

The Southerners surrendered Fort Henry. There was little fighting. Fort Donelson was stronger. Without waiting for orders, Sam decided to attack.

Sam rode through the woods toward the fort. He wanted to see it so he could make a plan. It was very cold.

When he got back to his soldiers, Sam was cheerful. "We can capture the fort," he told them.

Sam asked Navy gunboats to help. "Go up the river," he said. "Fire cannonballs at the fort."

Sam led his soldiers through the woods.

The Southerners in the fort fought bravely. But the gunboats and Sam's soldiers had them under heavy fire.

Suddenly, the Southerners burst out of the fort. Many of Sam's soldiers had not fought in a battle before. They were frightened and started to run away.

Sam saw a prisoner. He looked in the man's pack and found it full of food.

Sam leaped on Fox's back and galloped after his soldiers. "Stop!" he cried. "If the Southerners were attacking they would not carry so much food. They are trying to run away."

The Union soldiers stopped. They turned and captured the fort.

When President Lincoln heard that Sam had taken both forts he was happy.

During the next few months, Sam led his soldiers in other battles. Some of the older officers did not like Sam. "Grant should not be a general," they told Lincoln. "Too many soldiers are killed in his battles."

Lincoln shook his head. *"I can't spare this man,"* he said. *"He fights."*

Chapter 8

Sam's Bold Idea

The Southerners had the strongest fort in America. It was built around the city of Vicksburg, Mississippi. Sam decided to capture it. People said, "Grant cannot capture the fort. It's impossible to get at it."

The fort was across the wide Mississippi River. North of it were swamps. Cannons stood on the hills along the river. Behind the city were miles of trenches.

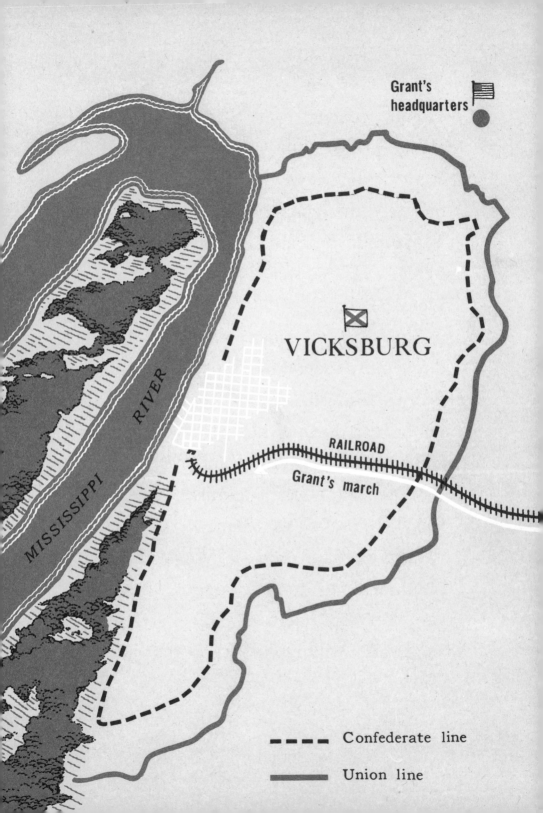

Grant's
headquarters

VICKSBURG

MISSISSIPPI RIVER

RAILROAD

Grant's march

- - - - Confederate line
——— Union line

Sam tried every idea he could think of to take the fort. Nothing seemed to work. The months wore on. A newspaperman wrote, "Grant is stupid." Sam's soldiers did not agree. They were ready to try any idea he had.

Sam's next idea was bold and dangerous. He talked it over with a Navy admiral. "Can you sail your gunboats down the river at night? Can you get by the cannons?"

"Yes, sir," the admiral said. He was as brave as Sam.

"Fine," Sam said. "We will march our men to meet you. Then you can ferry us across."

"I am willing to try," the admiral said.

The admiral asked for volunteers to sail the boats. Many of Sam's men volunteered. "We are not afraid," they said.

Mrs. Grant and her two oldest boys were visiting the army camp. Grant took them out in a small boat to watch the gunboats start down the river. It was a warm April night. The gunboats looked like huge, black shadows on the water.

Suddenly, a Southerner saw one. He set an old house on fire so he could see better. Eleven gunboats were in the middle of the river.

The Southerners lit bonfires. The fires made the night as bright as day. The Southerners ran to their cannons. The cannons roared.

Cannonballs hit every gunboat but only one ship sank. The rest swept safely past Vicksburg.

The next night, Sam and the admiral sent more boats down the river. Then Sam kissed Julia and the boys good-by. Fred, the oldest boy, said to him, "I am twelve years old. I want to go with you."

"All right," Sam said. He gave Fred a red sash and a sword, and a white horse to ride.

Gunboats ferried Sam's army across the river. There Sam spoke to a corporal. "Now you take care of Fred. I want him to be safe."

Sam marched his men against the fort. The Southerners in the trenches fought hard. So did Sam's soldiers.

Many of them died. Sam felt terrible.

He placed his men in a circle around the fort. No food could get in. The people of Vicksburg suffered. They even ate mules and rats. Finally the fort surrendered on July 4, 1863. Sam's soldiers whooped for joy. Sam was happy, too, but he was quiet.

The big river was now controlled by the United States. The Southerners could no longer get food from their western states.

Sam's bold idea helped the Union. Mr. Lincoln wrote Sam and thanked him. Congress voted Sam a gold medal. The President now knew that General Grant was one of his best leaders.

Chapter *9*

Sam Wins Again

After capturing Vicksburg, Sam took a steamboat to New Orleans. There the soldiers gave him a parade. Sam rode a borrowed horse. The band played gaily. The Union soldiers marched smartly. Suddenly, a railroad engine puffed by. The horse was frightened. Then it jumped and fell, pinning Sam underneath it. Sam's leg was badly hurt. He was in great pain.

Sam was in bed when a telegram came from Mr. Lincoln. It told him to come back north. Sam asked the doctors for help. They placed him on a stretcher and carried him to a river boat.

In Indiana, Sam met Lincoln's Secretary of War. "Go to Chattanooga, Tennessee, at once," Sam was told. "The Southerners have a Union army bottled up there. It is in danger."

The long ride across country was painful. It was hard for Sam to stick in the saddle. The soldiers riding with him took care of him. When they came to a bad place in the road they stopped. They lifted Sam from the saddle and carried him on their shoulders.

At Chattanooga, Sam saw that the Union soldiers could not fight until they had more food. He helped work out a plan to bring food to the city. When it arrived, the soldiers yelled, "Hooray for Grant!"

They took off their hats when Sam rode among them.

Many Southerners were on the hills above Chattanooga. Lookout Mountain and Missionary Ridge were crowded with their guns.

Sam waited for more Northern soldiers to arrive. Then he sent his men into the mountains. Deadly gunfire rained down from above. But Sam's men plunged into it. Their battle line was two miles long. They fought the Southerners hand-to-hand.

They forced the Southerners to retreat.

Sam's leadership had brought another great victory. He was famous now. People said that he should be President. Sam shook his head. "We have a fine President," he said.

Newspapermen came to see Sam, but they learned little from him. He was modest. He did not wish to talk about himself. "I just want to help win the war," he said. "Let's get the United States back together again."

Chapter *10*

U. S. Grant and Robert E. Lee

A few months later Mr. Lincoln sent for Sam. People in Washington were eager to see him. They crowded the White House. The tall President and the short general stood side by side.

Lincoln promoted Sam to be the head of all the armies of the United States. Sam was very pleased with the promotion. Twenty years had gone by since he stood on parade at West Point.

He remembered his secret dream. He was now the leader of one-half million soldiers.

"You have a hard time ahead," the President said. *"To win the war you must defeat General Lee's army. How are you going to do it?"*

Lee commanded a strong army in Virginia. He was the South's most famous general. But Grant was not afraid of him. He remembered meeting Lee years ago in Mexico.

Sam said, "Mr. President, I will lead the attack against Lee myself. We will never let up. I will have the rest of our armies attack elsewhere. The Southerners will be kept busy on all fronts. This will prevent them from sending help to Lee."

"Good," Mr. Lincoln said. *"The country trusts you."*

Soon some of the world's hardest battles were fought. One, the Battle of the Wilderness, was dreadful. Wounded men in both armies burned to death when the woods caught fire.

Sam kept his army hammering at Lee's army. He gave neither army time to rest. *"I propose to fight it out on this line if it takes all summer,"* he said.

During one battle, Sam sat on a log and wrote an order. A cannonball exploded at his feet. Luckily he was not hurt. The soldiers noticed that Sam had not even looked up. *"Ulysses doesn't scare worth a darn,"* they said.

A horrible battle took place at Cold Harbor, Virginia. Lee's army was in strong trenches. Sam marched his soldiers through the woods, straight at them. Thousands of Sam's men were killed. He felt badly because so many of his men died.

Sam did not stop. He marched his soldiers around Lee's army toward Petersburg, Virginia. Sam wanted to capture the railroads there. If he could do this, Lee's army could no longer get food.

Lee's army pulled back near Petersburg. Both armies dug trenches and fought each other from them.

At the end of a year, Lee's army could no longer stand the terrible strain. His men were worn out.

Some of them left for home. Soon Sam had Lee surrounded. Lee saw that he could not win. He sent a white flag to Sam. It was a flag of surrender.

The two leaders met on April 9, 1865. They entered a farmhouse at Appomattox Court House, Virginia. Lee wore a new, gray uniform. He carried a sword of gold. His boots shone. Sam wore an old, blue uniform. It had three stars sewed to each shoulder. His shoes were muddy. "I've been too busy to clean up," Sam explained.

The two leaders sat down, each at a table. Sam wrote a paper giving the terms of surrender. He said the war in Virginia was over. Lee's soldiers would not be put in prison.

They could go home and take their horses with them. Lee signed his name agreeing to the surrender. It was an important moment in American history.

Lee said, "My soldiers are starving. They have had little to eat."

Sam felt sorry for the Southerners. He wanted to do everything he could to end the hard feelings caused by the war. Sam made sure that Lee's soldiers received food.

The two generals shook hands. They walked out of the farmhouse and said good-by to each other. Grant raised his hat in salute to Lee.

Every man present was thankful that the terrible war was almost over. Sam's soldiers cheered him loudly.

They fired guns in salute. "Stop that!" Sam said. *"There will be no crowing. The Southerners are our enemies no longer."*

Everywhere in America church bells tolled. The day was Palm Sunday, 1865.

Chapter *11*

President Sam Grant

Five days after Lee surrendered, Abraham Lincoln was shot. Thousands mourned his death. Sam felt crushed. He had lost a friend.

Many of the Northern leaders wanted to punish the South. The new President, Andrew Johnson, could do little to stop them. Hatred spread over the country again. This worried Sam. He wanted to see the country united and everyone friendly.

When the time came to elect another President, people thought of Sam Grant. "He was one of our greatest generals," they said. "He was fair. He would make a fine President."

While the election was being held, Sam went back home to Galena, Illinois. The people in Galena were proud of Sam. They gave him a house. When he was elected President they were very happy. So were thousands of men who had been his soldiers.

It was truly an amazing story. The clerk in the Galena leather store had become a world-famous general, and now was the President of the United States.

Sam moved his wife and children to the White House. His oldest son, Fred, was nineteen. Mrs. Grant helped Sam in his wish to live simply. But he had to go to many parties and he did not like them. He was shy. At one party he said to a lady, *"Madam, I had rather storm a fort than attempt another dance."*

Sam found the presidency a hard job. He hoped to rebuild the South as soon as possible. The last of the Southern states did rejoin the Union in 1870, and Sam was pleased. The Negroes were given the right to vote that year, too. But this did not mean an end to trouble in the South.

Northern soldiers were still stationed there. The Southerners disliked this.

And they did not like the dishonest Northerners who wormed their way into their state governments. The Southerners did everything they could to keep the Negroes from voting. There was bitterness and terror.

Sam Grant wanted all the troubles stopped. But he did not know how to go about it. By mistake, he often helped the people who were making it hard for the Southerners.

Sam was elected President another time. His troubles grew still worse. Businessmen who were friends cheated the government. Other friends he had appointed to government offices turned out to be dishonest, too. Sam Grant was honest. But sometimes he trusted the wrong people.

Sam was a poor President, but it was not entirely his fault. He did not understand politics. His army experience did not help him. He had not been trained in government.

He was able to do some good things. He smoothed over a quarrel with England. He put an end to high prices. He lowered taxes. He saw the nation united again. That was most important.

When Sam left the White House, he and his wife and their youngest son traveled around the world. Huge crowds everywhere wanted to see the great American general. Kings and queens gave parties for the Grants. In India, Sam, the splendid horseman, rode elephants.

When Sam grew older he wrote the story of his life. This was hard to do because he became very ill. But it is a great book.

Sam died in 1885. The entire country mourned his death. With Abraham Lincoln, Sam had saved the Union.

A tomb was built for Sam's body in New York City. It is on a hill above the Hudson, thirty-five miles down the river from West Point. On the walls of the tomb is a message he gave twice to the nation: *"Let us have peace."*

1133